DAVID PAUL WERNER

Eleven Chorale Settings

for Organ

Christian Arts Foundation

ISBN 978-988-18820-4-2

Published by Christian Arts Foundation, www.caf.org.hk

Performance notes

THREE PASSION PRELUDES were inspired by each prelude's Scriptural epigraph:

+ the mocking torment inflicted on Jesus, described in Matthew 27:29-30 (Bicinium: Passion Chorale)

+ the wondrous depiction of elders singing before the Lamb, in Revelation 5:8-9 (Canticle: *O Lamm Gottes unschuldig*)

+ the assuring yet fearsome prophesy of redemption and justice, Isaiah 59:19-20 (Prélude-Étude: The King's Majesty)

PRELUDE ON *ABERYSTWYTH* was first improvised on a 3-manual instrument, given here as a registration option.

THREE VARIATIONS ON *TON-Y-BOTEL* (EBENEZER) are pastoral, whimsical and melodramatic, respectively. In the spirit of the tune's frivolous moniker (Tune in a Bottle) variations 2 and 3 are better suited for entertainment than ecclesiastical use.

Registration: Suggestions herein are for a quintessential 2-manual church organ (exemplified below) serving as liberal guides to timbre, balance and overarching effect.

Notation conventions:

· Common notes passing from one voice to another are often not shown as tied, but in legato playing are to be tied unless [1] a rearticulation (/) is explicitly indicated, or [2] it would result in a tie to a descending melodic line on the same manual.

· Dynamics from *pp* to *f* indicate relative position of expression shutters, from fully closed to fully open.

· Wedges ($<$ $>$) or text *cresc.* and *dim.* indicate gradual opening and closing of expression shutters.

· +Reg. and −Reg. means to add and remove registers (*i.e.*, stops), respectively.

· *ff* indicates full or relatively full organ with expression shutters open.

· Divisional abbreviations are G or Gt. for Great (primary manual), S or Sw. for Swell (subordinate manual) and Ped. for Pedal.

· GS on manual staves means play on Great with Swell coupled.

· G, S or GS on the pedal staff indicates which manuals are to be coupled to the pedal.

· Solo on the pedal staff means no manual-to-pedal couplers are engaged.

D. P. W.

First Presbyterian Church, Wonju, Korea
Beckerath, 2006

Hauptwerk	Schwellwerk	Pedal
8′ Principal	8′ Rohrflöte	16′ Subbaß
8′ Spielflöte	8′ Salicional	8′ Octavbaß
4′ Oktave	4′ Hohlflöte	8′ Offenflöte
4′ Spitzflöte	II Sesquialtera	4′ Choralbaß
2²/₃′ Quinte	2′ Principal	IV Rauschpfeife
2′ Offenflöte	IV Scharf	16′ Fagott
V Mixtur	8′ Hautbois	
8′ Trompete		

St. Andrew Lutheran Church, Beaverton OR, USA
Fritts, 1993

Man. I	Man. II	Pedal
16′ Quintadena	8′ Rohrflöte	16′ Subbaß
8′ Principal	8′ Gemshorn	8′ Principal
8′ Rohrflöte	4′ Spitzgedackt	8′ Gedackt
4′ Octav	2′ Waldflöte	4′ Octav
2²/₃′ Nasat (half)	1¹/₃′ Sifflöte	16′ Posaune
II Cornet (full)	8′ Trichterregal	8′ Trompet
2′ Octav		
IV Mixtur		
8′ Trompet		

THREE PASSION PRELUDES

David Paul Werner

Bicinium: Passion Chorale

A crown of thorns they put on his head, and a reed in his right hand.
They mocked him, saying, "Hail, king of the Jews!" They spat
on him, and they took the reed and struck him on the head.

R.h.: Keening, plaintive
L.h.: Heavy, but with definition

Quasi agitato, ma senza fretta ♩=52

2.
arabesco libero
7
rall. poco a poco
largamente
(r.h.)

Canticle: O Lamm Gottes unschuldig

*The elders, holding golden vials full and fragrant with the prayers
of saints, bowed down before the lamb, singing a new song: "Worthy
are you who was slain; who, by your blood, has redeemed us to God…"*

R.h.: Brilliant, penetrating
L.h.: Richly-toned 8'
Ped.: Fundamental 16'

Più lento ♩=54
2.
(Hæc dies)
(Sanctus)
Ped. +Reed 16' or 8'

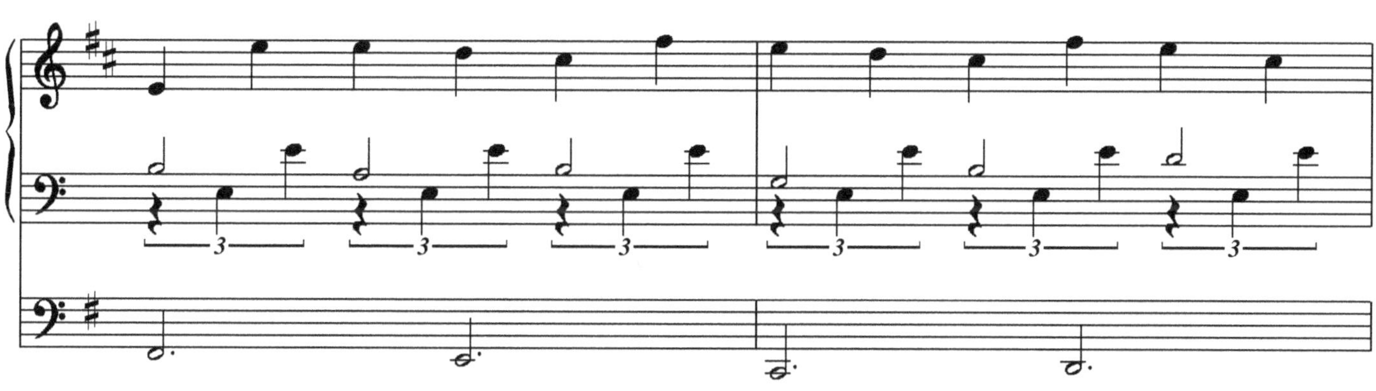

riten.
Quasi tempo I°
poco rall.
Ped. —Reed

Prélude-Étude: The King's Majesty

They shall fear the name of the Lord from the west, and his glory from
the rising of the sun; for he will come like a rushing stream, which the
wind of the Lord drives. And he will come to Zion as Redeemer…

Gt.: Flutes, Bourdons 8' (4')
Sw.: Full (less if unexpressed)
Ped.: 16' 8', Reed 8' or 16'

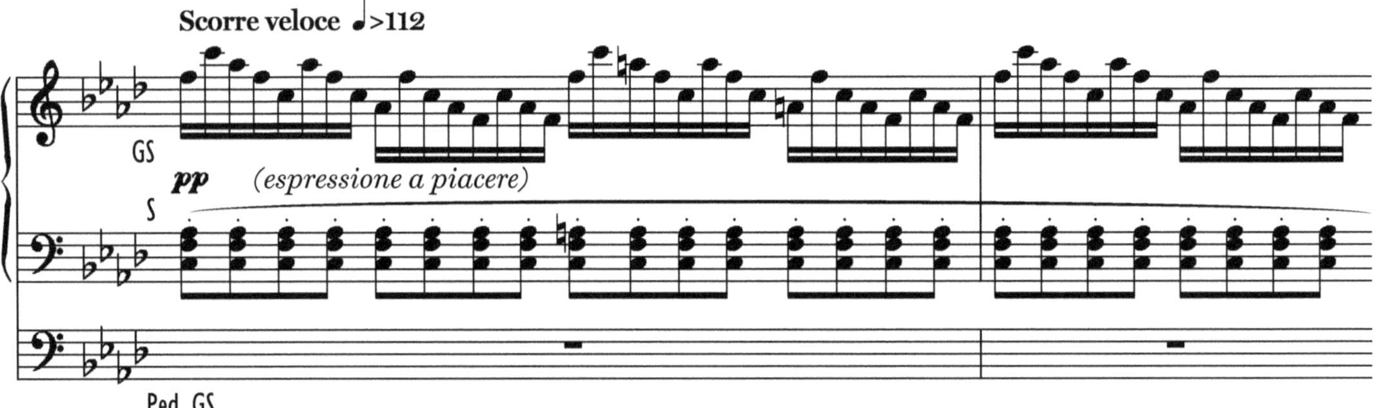

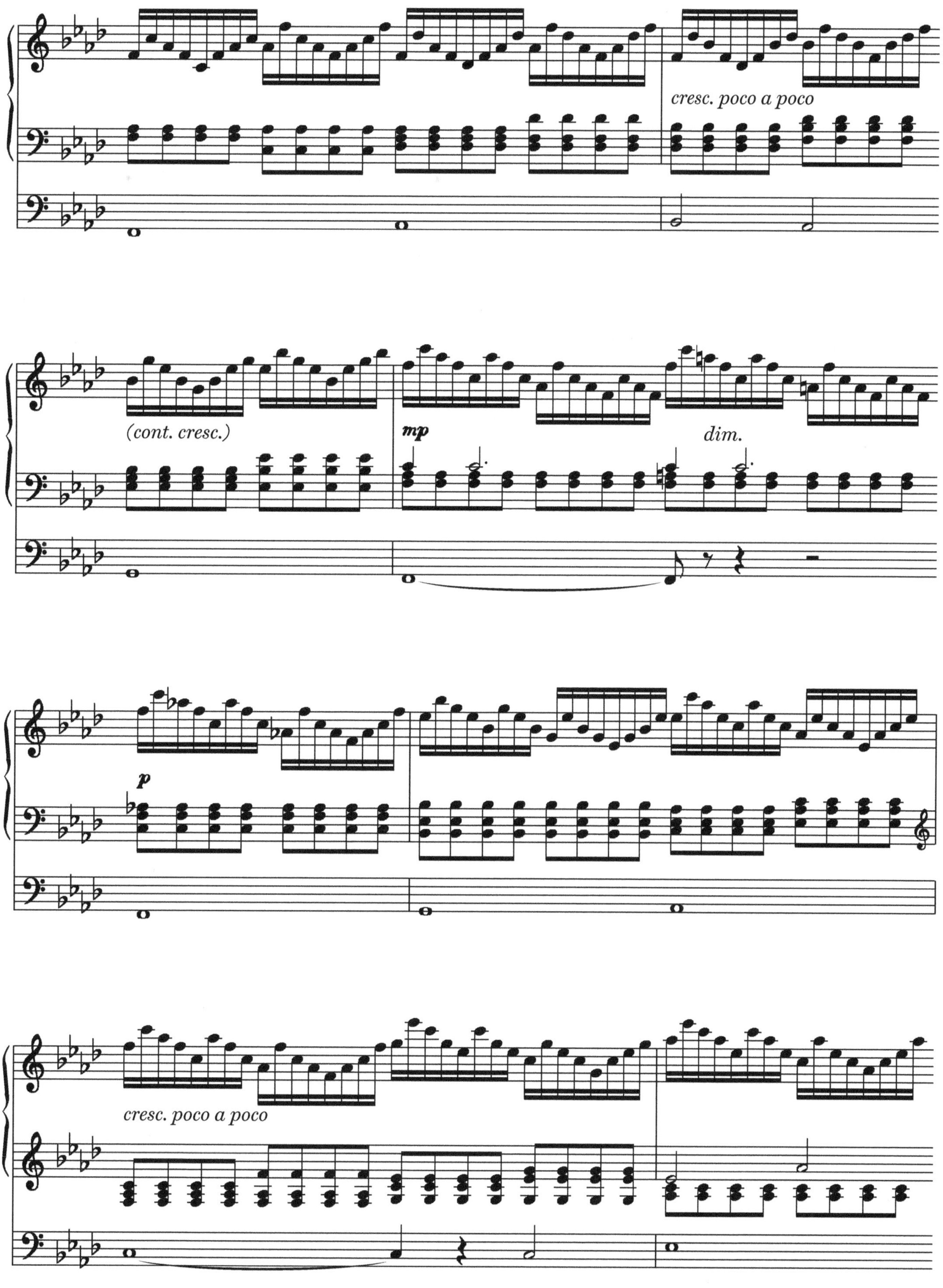

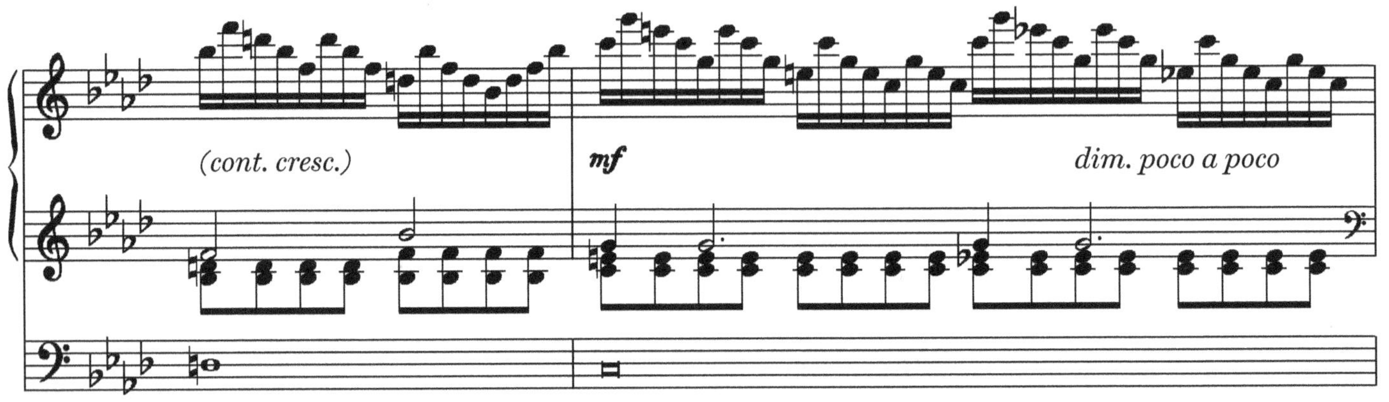
(cont. cresc.)
mf
dim. poco a poco

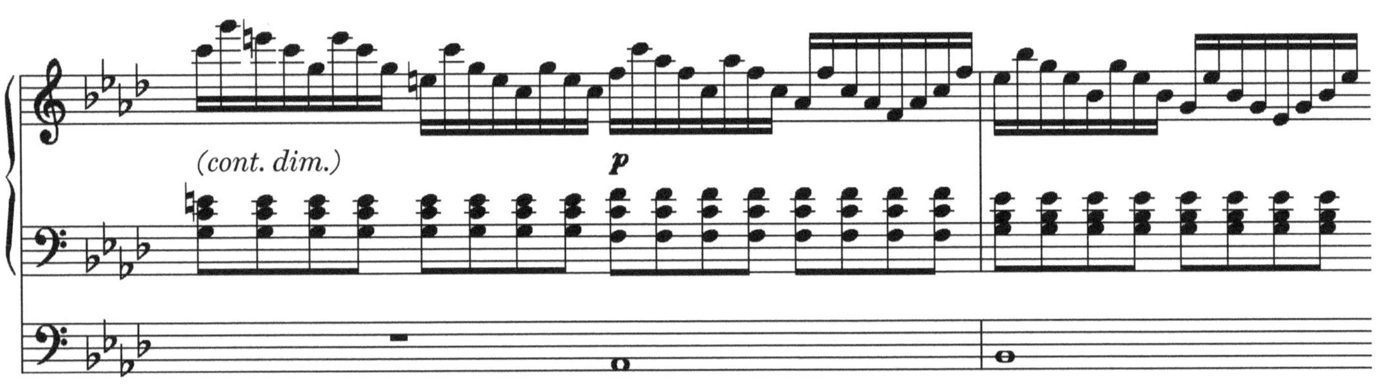
(cont. dim.)
p

cresc. poco a poco

(cont. cresc.)
f

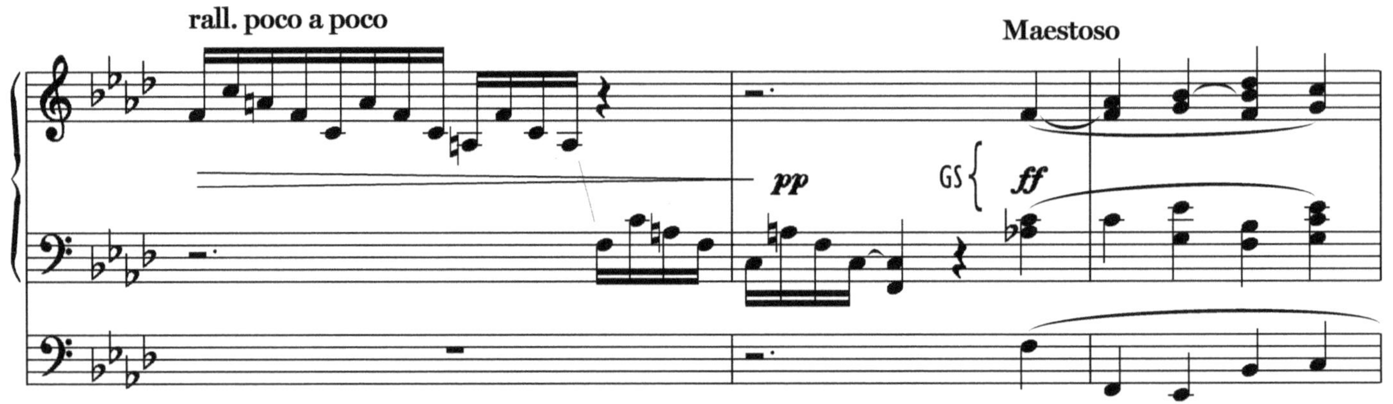

rall. poco a poco
Maestoso
pp
GS
ff

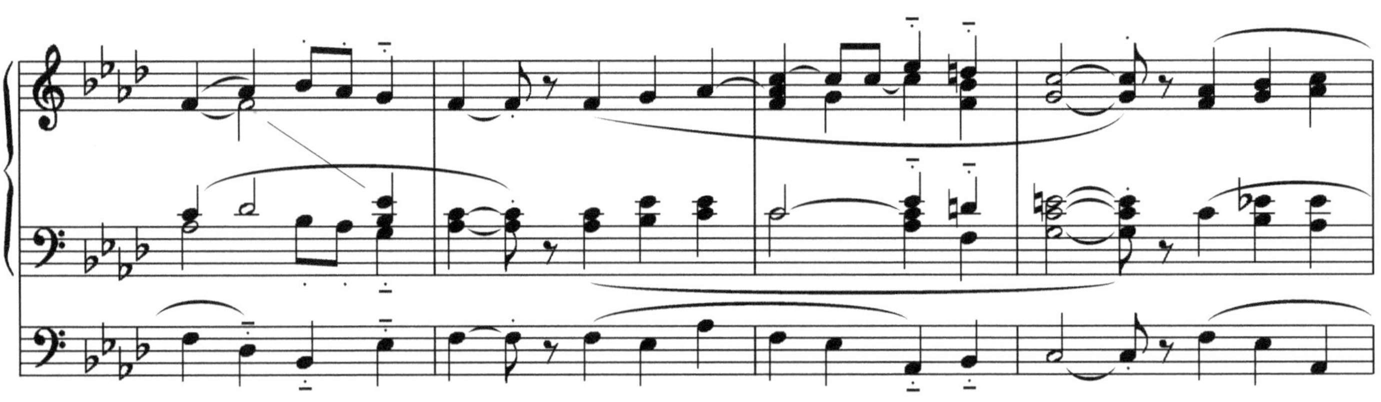

rall. poco a poco
riten.
più larga

Three Chorale Versets

from the "The Trees Shall Sing!"

David Paul Werner

1. Chesterfield

in canon at the fourth

Gt.: Flute 8', with Octave, 12th or Sesquialtera
Sw.: Mild Foundations 8' 4'
Ped.: Bourdon 16', with Principal 8' or 4'

2. Lobe den Herren

Gt.: Full, smooth tone, e.g., Diapason and Bourdon 8'
Sw.: Ethereal, e.g., Voix célestes II, Soft 4'
Ped.: Soft 16', Sw./Ped.

3. Old Hundredth

With full organ at Andante maestoso,
or softly luminous at Largo sostenuto.

Two Devotional Interludes

Prayer

*I saw the Spirit descending from heaven
like a dove, and it abode upon Him.*

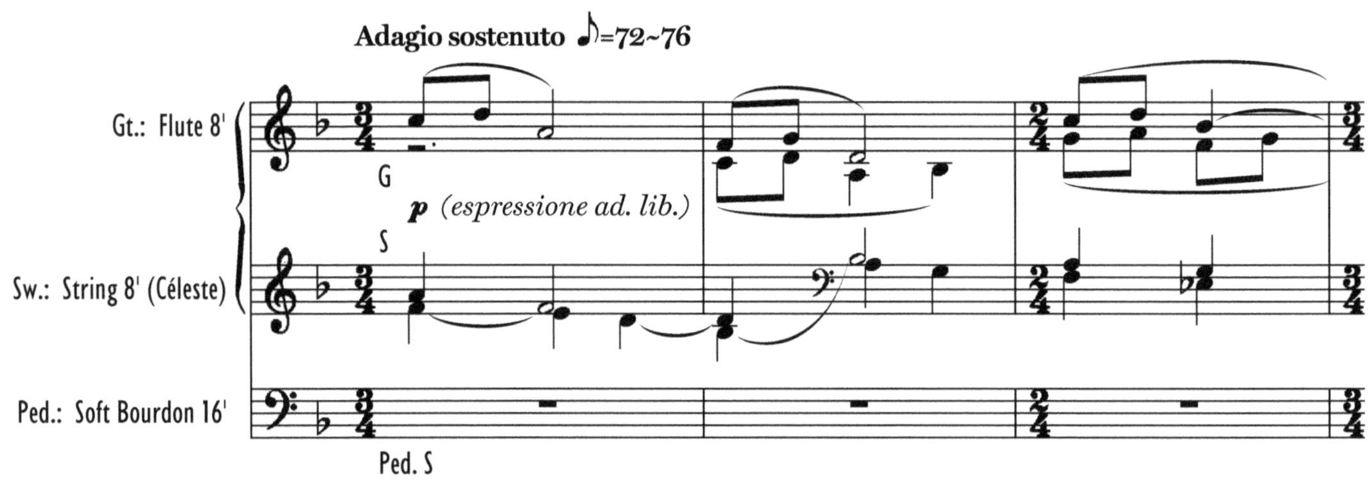

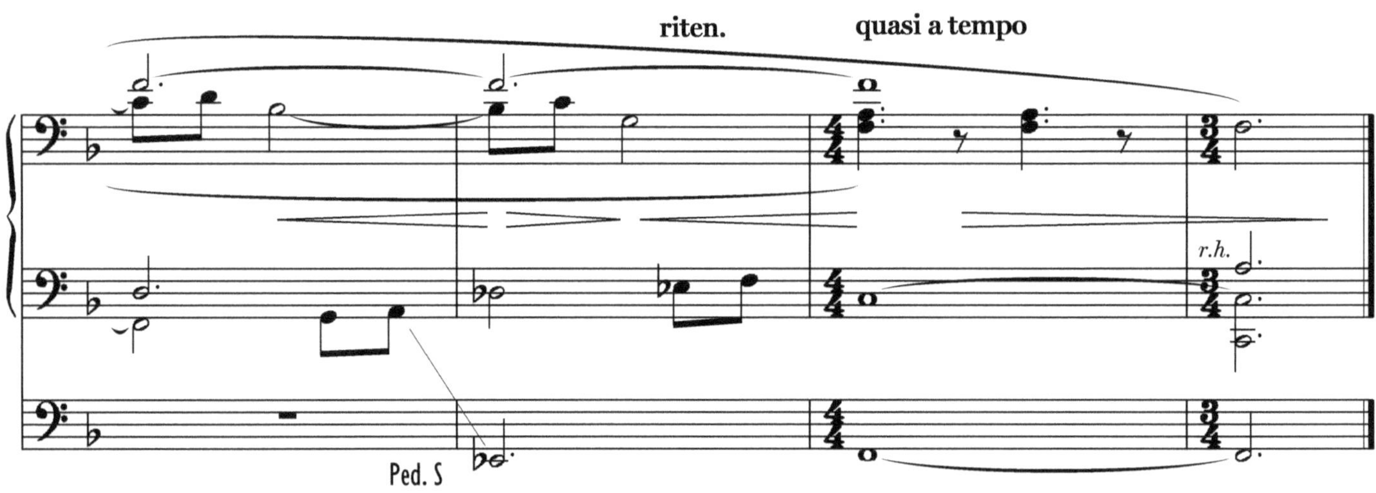

Adagietto

from "Toccata Concertino"

(alternate key in Addendum)

Gt.: Melodious diapason or flute tone; opt. trem. if no Sw. céleste

Sw.: Light foundations 8'; opt. céleste

Alt. reg. – Gt.: Bourdon 16'; play one octave higher than written

Sw.: Voix célestes II

Preludes on "Aberystwyth"

David Paul Werner

Original version – Tune melismatically obscured

Gt.: Diapason or Flute 8'
(Ch.: Soft 8' coupled to Gt.)
Sw.: Foundations 8' (opt. Céleste, Nazard)
Ped.: Bourdon 16'

mf
r.h.
p
cresc. poco a poco
3
f
GS
(CS)
s
dim. poco a poco fino alla fine
riten.
(S)

Gt.: Mild 8'
Sw.: Foundations 8' (opt. Céleste)
Ped.: Bourdon 16'

Three Variations on "Ton-y-Botel"

("Ebenezer")

1. Alaw

(Air)

David Paul Werner

Gt.: Mild Foundation(s) 8' (4')
Sw.: Dulcet Cornet or Reed
Ped.: 8' to balance Gt.

a tempo
S
G 1° reg.
Ped. 1° reg.
esitare   Quasi tempo 1°
G
Ped.
2. Mympwy
(Caprice)
Allegro giocoso
8' 2'
sempre staccatissimo
3
3
1.
3
3

2.
1.
2. poco più lento

3. Ymdaith Angladd

(Cortège)

Gt.: Foundations 8' 4' 2' (no Mix.)
Sw.: Full, without 16'
Ped.: Foundations 16' 8' 4'

Tempo I°
S { mp
GS { pp
cresc.
legato
Reduce Ped. to Bourdons 16' 8' solo
quasi pizzicato
Ped. S + Foundations

allargando poco a poco
(cont. cresc.)
ff
+ Gt. Reeds
Ped. GS + Reeds

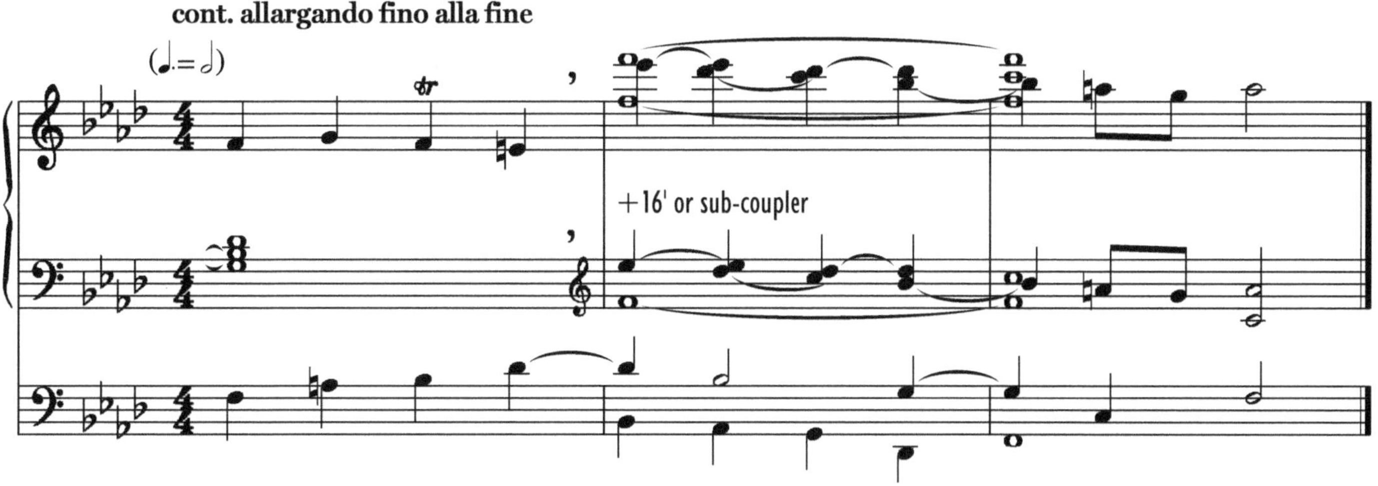

cont. allargando fino alla fine
+ 16' or sub-coupler

Addendum

Adagietto from "Toccata Concertino"
(alternate version in B minor)

Man. I : Bourdon 16', or Flute(s) 8' (4'); Man. II/Man. I; opt. Trem.;
      with Bourdon 16' play one octave higher

Man. II: Light 8', *e.g.*, Salicional or Gemshorn

Ped. :   Man. II/Ped.

teneramente
rall.
più adagio
Coupler off